a journal

Make Time
BE PRESENT

Meditations to Be Here Now

erika kearns

Castle Point Books
New York

www.stmartins.com
www.castlepointbooks.com

The Castle Point Books trademark is owned by Castle Point Publications, LLC.
Castle Point books are published and distributed by St. Martin's Press.

ISBN 978-1-250-21621-2 (trade paperback)

Cover design by Katie Jennings Campbell
Interior design by Joanna Williams

Images used under license from Shutterstock.com

Our books may be purchased in bulk for promotional, educational, or business
use. Please contact your local bookseller or the Macmillan Corporate and
Premium Sales Department at 1-800-221-7945, extension 5442, or by email at
MacmillanSpecialMarkets@macmillan.com.

First Edition: August 2019

10 9 8 7 6 5 4 3 2 1

THIS JOURNAL BELONGS TO

You must live in the
PRESENT,
launch yourself on
every wave,
find your eternity
in each
MOMENT.

—Henry David Thoreau

So much competes for your attention each day

that your life can feel a little like whiplash. But what if it could be different? Imagine yourself fully focused and engaged in each moment and naturally calm and confident in who you are and the choices you make. You've already taken the first step toward that new picture by picking up this journal.

Make Time, Be Present encourages a life-changing mindfulness practice with meditations and exercises that take just minutes and can be incorporated into pockets of time throughout your day. Each page is designed to help you find paths to greater joy in the present moment. You'll discover how to acknowledge what you're feeling when you feel it and tools to help you free yourself from emotional places where you don't want to stay. Mindfulness meditation can help you:

- Reduce anxiety
- Nurture self-acceptance
- Strengthen relationships
- Sleep better
- Improve attention and memory
- Simply enjoy life more!

Use this journal as a quiet place to center your thoughts and find the meditation techniques that work best for you. There's no one correct path—just jump in where you feel led and revisit pages as you'd like over and over again. Whenever you feel disconnected, find your clear mind again with *Make Time, Be Present.*

CLEARING THE STORM

What are the random thoughts or worries swirling around inside your head today, distracting you from what really matters in the moment? Write them here.

Now take a snow globe and shake it vigorously—in real life or simply in your mind. Set it down gently and watch as everything settles into a clear state again. Focus your mind to follow, as your storm of thoughts and emotions calms.

The day she
LET GO
of the things that
were weighing her down
was the day she began
TO SHINE
the brightest.

—Katrina Mayer

The soul
becomes dyed with
the color of its

THOUGHTS.

—Marcus Aurelius

USING COLOR CUES

What do you need more of today—energy, calm, confidence, joy, healing? Choose a color that speaks that quality to you:

As you go through your day, look for that color in your environment when you need focus. Stop and study an object of that color as if seeing it for the first time. How does the color meditation affect your day?

SIMPLE STARFISH MEDITATION

Reconnect with a sense of calm by stretching out one hand and spreading your fingers wide. Using the pointer finger of your other hand, gently trace the outline of the outstretched fingers, taking time to travel completely up and down each finger. Think of a five-word phrase or sentence that you can silently say as you round each finger. Try out a few possibilities here.

1. _____

2. _____

3. _____

4. _____

5. _____

1. _____

2. _____

3. _____

4. _____

5. _____

1. _____

2. _____

3. _____

4. _____

5. _____

COMING HOME

Setting aside just a few minutes to focus on an object or a simple task when you arrive home each day can anchor you in your surroundings. What will your anchor be? Draw it here.

Having spent the better
part of my life trying either
to relive the past or

EXPERIENCE

the future before it arrives,
I have come to believe that in
between these two extremes is

PEACE.

—Anonymous

We have to get back to

THE BEAUTY

of just being alive in this
present moment.

—Mary McDonnell

DISTRACTIONS DOWN THE DRAIN

Anxieties can weigh on your mind and rob you of opportunities for presence and joy. What is burdening you unnecessarily today?

As you go through your day, imagine your sources of anxiety disappearing down the drain every time you wash your hands. Let the fresh water cleanse your thoughts and awaken you to fully appreciate what your senses are experiencing in each new moment, without lingering on the past or jumping into the future.

MEETING THE MORNING

Consider what the first ten minutes of your day look and feel like. How could you better awaken your senses and set the tone for a more mindful day? What are the first things you want to ...

... feel?

... hear?

... see?

... smell?

... taste?

When you arise in the
morning, think of what

A PRECIOUS
PRIVILEGE

it is to be alive—
to breathe, to think,
to enjoy, to love.

–Marcus Aurelius

Do the

HEART-WORK

on the images
imprisoned within you.

—Rainer Maria Rilke

REMOVING THE BARRIERS

Insecurities can block enjoyment of the present. You may tell yourself that you don't deserve peace, fulfillment, or happiness, or that you haven't earned better yet. Reject the lies by completing the sentences below with the positive truths you know when you look deeper.

In this present moment, I am

In this present moment, I am

In this present moment, I am

In this present moment, I am

In this present moment,
I am *enough*.

BACK-TO-THE-PRESENT BODY SCAN

While sitting or lying down, focus on each area of your body
and the sensations you are feeling, starting at your feet. If any
area feels tense or heavy, let it soften or lighten. Are your toes
clenched? Release them. Is your back tight? Relax it into the
surface it's touching. Where did you sense the most tension?

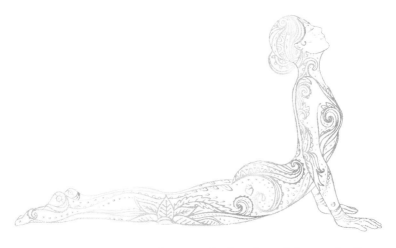

How did your mind feel when your body released the tension?

It's not the
LOAD
that breaks you down,
it's the way you
CARRY IT.

—Lou Holtz

That's why people
LISTEN TO MUSIC
or look at paintings.
To get in touch with that
WHOLENESS.

—Corita Kent

LISTENING DEEPER

Choose a song that you find calming. Try to listen to it as if you're hearing it for the first time. As you listen, record every unique instrument you hear.

CLEAR SKIES

What thoughts are clouding your head right now? Write them on the clouds and imagine them floating. Decide what to do with each thought—for example, let negative thoughts pass with the wind or try to see them from a new perspective that's less threatening.

You are

THE SKY.

Everything else is just

THE WEATHER.

—Pema Chödrön

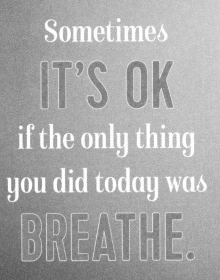

Sometimes
IT'S OK
if the only thing
you did today was
BREATHE.

–Anonymous

VALUE IN EVERY MOMENT

Sometimes it's okay to just be . . . okay. Not every experience or result is going to be a wow moment. When you only honor those mountaintops, you can lose sight of some beautiful little peaks along the way—and the expectations for what qualifies as significant get almost unreachable. What went okay for you today? (Nothing is too insignificant!)

THANKFUL FOR THE MOMENTS

Throughout your day, notice and show gratitude for all the people in your life who serve you—in big or little ways. Note a few and how they serve you here.

It is through

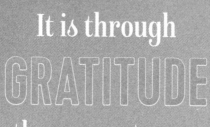

GRATITUDE

for the present moment
that the spiritual

DIMENSION

of life opens up.

—Eckhart Tolle

You must be
completely awake in
THE PRESENT
to enjoy the tea.

—Thich Nhat Hanh

TRUE TASTES

Slow down and savor the first three bites of every food you eat today. Notice the food's texture, temperature, and flavor, what it brings to mind, and what feelings it inspires. Record your observations here.

Breakfast:

Lunch:

Dinner:

CLEARING THE CLUTTER

When you're surrounded by environmental chaos and disorder, it can carry over to your mental state. What ten things can you clear away or get rid of to create more space for everyday mindfulness in your surroundings?

1. _____

2. _____

3. _____

4. _____

5. _____

6. _____

7. _____

8. _____

9. _____

10. _____

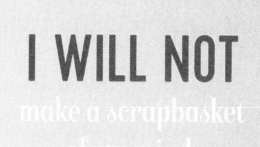

I WILL NOT

make a scrapbasket
of my mind.

—Anonymous

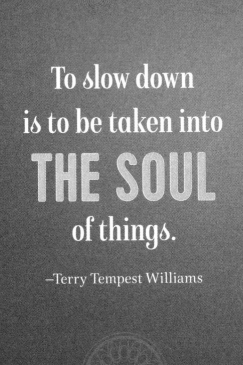

To slow down
is to be taken into
THE SOUL
of things.

–Terry Tempest Williams

RECOGNIZING "JUST THOUGHTS"

Traveling inside the mind can be like driving multiple cars at the same time down a high-speed highway without guardrails. To help slow down and bring your mind and body into the present reality, jot down all the random traffic racing through your mind right now.

Now, write "just thoughts" on a few small pieces of tape and cover every thought you released above.

HEART CONNECTION

Close your eyes and take a series of deep breaths. When you're ready, while continuing to breathe deeply, move one hand over your heart. Bring the other hand on top. Feel your heart grow full on the in-breath and soften on the out-breath. What are you grateful for in this moment? Can you hold on to that feeling in your heart and mind throughout the rest of the day?

A few simple
TIPS FOR LIFE:
feet on the ground,
head to the skies,
heart open …
quiet mind.

—Rasheed Ogunlaru

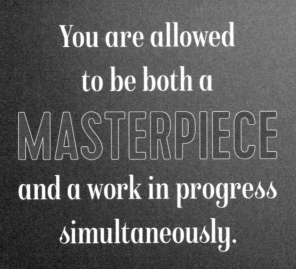

You are allowed
to be both a
MASTERPIECE
and a work in progress
simultaneously.

—Sophia Bush

EMOTIONS TO WORDS

Are you *frustrated, fearful, stressed, distracted?* Naming your emotions helps you first to acknowledge the mess you're feeling and then to look at the feelings in a more intellectual and less emotionally overwhelming way. Write in big, bold letters a word to describe any negative emotions you're feeling. Then write it a few more times, getting smaller and lighter as you move down the page.

PAUSING WITH NATURE

Find a small gift from nature, such as a leaf, an acorn, a seashell, or a flower petal. Really take it in with as many senses as you can. Sketch or write about what you notice when you study it closely.

When you take a
FLOWER
in your hand and really
look at it, it's your
WORLD
for the moment.

—Georgia O'Keeffe

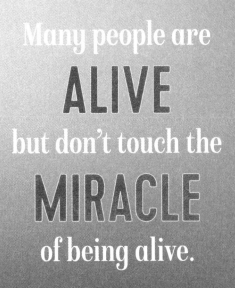

Many people are

ALIVE

but don't touch the

MIRACLE

of being alive.

–Thich Nhat Hanh

HANDS-ON HEALING

Use even a small pocket of time today to make or do something with your hands. Strum a guitar, knead bread dough, knit or crochet. Focus wholly on the process and not the outcome. How did you feel during and after?

SHEDDING REGRET

What regret from the past is it time to release? Leave it here so that you are once again open to new opportunities and enjoyment of the present.

Just as a snake
SHEDS ITS SKIN,
we must
SHED OUR PAST
over and over again.

—Buddha

That's life:
starting over,
ONE BREATH
at a time.

—Sharon Salzberg

TWO FEET, ONE BREATH

Identify situations in which you tend to get swept away by
negative emotions.

The next time you enter one of those tough places, try this
technique: simply stop to feel your two feet rooted in the ground
and take one conscious deep breath.

FINDING THE SUN

Whether you are inside or outside, find a private spot of sun where you can bask in its warmth with your eyes closed. When you open your eyes after this pause, write what words come to mind.

The
SUN SHINES
not on us but
IN US.

—John Muir

Slow breathing
is like an

ANCHOR

in the midst
of an emotional

STORM.

—Russ Harris

BREATHING BUDDY

Find something that you can place comfortably on your stomach—a small pillow, a stuffed animal, or even a stone will work well. Lie down on your back with the object in place. Focus your attention fully on the rise and fall of the "buddy" as you inhale deeply through your nose, filling your belly with air, and then exhale slowly. Repeat this belly breathing sequence ten times.

Do you feel different after the exercise?

DRAWING YOUR CIRCLE

Close your eyes and summon a picture of all the people in your life who accept you as you are. Open your eyes and draw them or write their names in a circle.

I know that
the purpose of life is to

UNDERSTAND

and be in the present moment
with the people

YOU LOVE.

It's just that simple.

—Jane Seymour

Live being

TRUE

to the single

PURPOSE

of the moment.

–Yamamoto Tsunetomo

UNITASKING MISSION

Choose one activity—anything from washing dishes to walking in nature—that you will focus on doing mindfully in the next day. Aim to acknowledge stray thoughts that enter your mind, but then release them as efficiently as you can. To help keep your mind in the present, call upon your senses. What do you experience?

Sights

Sounds

Smells

Touches

Tastes

MOVIE MAKING

If the thoughts in your mind right now were a movie, what would the title be?

Imagine each thought passing as simply a scene on a screen. How do you feel as you face them from this perspective?

Start observing
your own mind.
Do not try to escape;
DO NOT BE AFRAID
of your thinking.

–Swami Rama

The little things?

THE LITTLE MOMENTS?

They aren't little.

—Jon Kabat-Zinn

APPRECIATION OF MOMENTS

Make a list of five "little" things or moments that have been memorable or have positively affected your life.

1. _____

_____

2. _____

_____

3. _____

_____

4. _____

_____

5. _____

_____

As you go through your day, notice how many of these little moments you encounter that you may not have noticed before.

COURT RECESS

Mindfulness is noticing what's happening in the present without judging. Notice where your judging mind takes you throughout your day.

What I saw

My initial reaction (judgment)

How I can think differently

The only
DIFFERENCE
between a flower
and a weed is
JUDGMENT.

—Wayne Dyer

The stiller
you are, the

CALMER

life is.

—Rasheed Ogunlaru

FLAME FOCUS

Light a candle that you can view comfortably at eye level. As you breathe slowly and deeply, focus your gaze on the candle's flame. Notice any colors, movement, scents, warmth, even gentle sounds given off by the candle. If negative thoughts come up, see them rising up from the candle and release them in the space below. Center thoughts of peace in the present moment in the flame.

SPONTANEOUS JOY

Surprise yourself with permission to do one thing you didn't expect to have time to do. For instance, connect with an old friend, take the scenic route, or look through favorite photos. What do you choose? How does it feel?

Life gives you

PLENTY OF TIME

to do whatever you want

to do if you stay in the

PRESENT MOMENT.

–Deepak Chopra

To be

CONTENT

with what one has
is the greatest
and truest of

RICHES.

—Cicero

GRATITUDE CHECK-IN

Schedule a midday time to pause for five minutes and meditate on all you are grateful for so far in your day. Set a reminder on your computer or phone to help you honor this time. Record your joys below.

CREATING A TRIGGER

Choose a routine activity that occurs at least a few times throughout your day. It could be washing your hands, starting your car, or flipping a light switch. Make it your reminder to take five to ten deep breaths and truly connect with your senses in the experience. How many times did the trigger prompt you? How did it feel?

If you cannot

FIND PEACE

within yourself,
you will never find it
anywhere else.

—Marvin Gaye

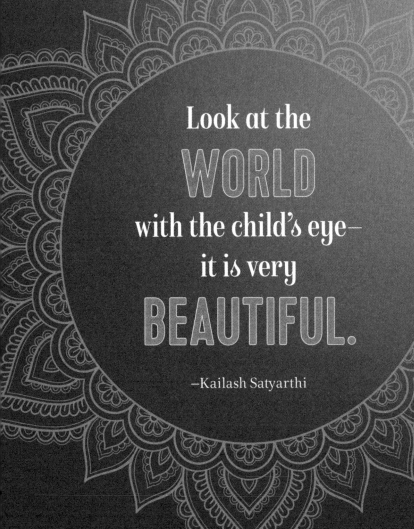

Look at the

WORLD

with the child's eye—
it is very

BEAUTIFUL.

—Kailash Satyarthi

THROUGH A CHILD'S EYES

Sometimes looking back can help you find more enjoyment in the present, if you do it wisely. Recall when you were a kid: what activity made you lose all track of time? What elements of that activity still stand out for you that you can enjoy in the now?

COOKING WITH INTENTION

Choose a meal you can prepare without time constraints. As you handle each ingredient, focus on everything you can sense about it (from color to aroma). Consider where each ingredient might have come from. Be mindful of how each kitchen tool you use helps you. Is your eating experience changed?

Every moment
nature is serving
fresh dishes with the items
OF HAPPINESS.
It is our choice to
recognize and taste it.

—Amit Ray

Each place is the

RIGHT PLACE—

the place where
I now am can be a

SACRED SPACE.

—Ravi Ravindra

EVERYDAY SACRED SPACES

Wherever you are, look around for sights you consider beautiful in this moment. Capture them in words or pictures below.

NATURAL GROUNDING

Standing on grass, soil, sand, or stone, take a deep breath in. Then exhale slowly and repeat two more times. Inhale deeply again, this time visualizing that you are drawing breath from the ground, through your feet and legs, and into your lungs. Exhale slowly, sending your breath back into the earth. Repeat several times. Which words capture how you feel? Circle them and add your own.

Aware   Connected   Renewed

Focused   Wise   Inspired

The more

GROUNDED

you are, the

HIGHER

you fly.

—J. R. Rim

You can clutch the past
so tightly to your chest that it
leaves your arms too full
TO EMBRACE
THE PRESENT.

—Jan Glidewell

DONE WITH THE DEBATE

What argument from an earlier encounter are you still battling in your head? In the space below, get out all the points you've been piling up since the actual event. Then leave them behind and breathe.

TURNING OFF AUTOPILOT

New experiences can awaken your senses. It could be as simple as sampling a different variety of coffee or listening to new music. What little detours from your usual routine can you take?

Straight lines go too

QUICKLY

to appreciate the

PLEASURES

of the journey.

—René Crevel

Open the

WINDOW

of your mind.
Allow the fresh air,
new lights and new

TRUTHS

to enter.

—Amit Ray

RECORDER TRANSFORMATION

Find a place where you can sit or lie comfortably and close your eyes. For a few minutes, truly listen without drawing conclusions about what you might be hearing. (For example, describe the birdcall you hear without trying to figure out what type of bird produced the sound.) Record what you hear below.

Were there sounds you picked up that you've never heard before in this place?

DIGITAL DETOX

Every time you reach for your phone today, pause, take a deep breath, and ask, "Can it wait?" If it honestly can, put the urge here in a parking lot until tomorrow, when you can reassess whether your phone grab was a distraction or a true need.

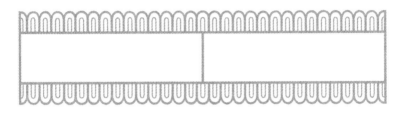

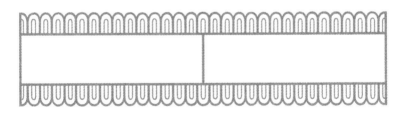

Don't gain the

WORLD

and lose your

SOUL.

—Bob Marley

Use every distraction
as an object of

MEDITATION

and they cease to be

distractions.

–Mingyur Rinpoche

MINDFUL DOODLING

Doodling can be a way to connect emotions with more structured thinking. Research finds that doodling boosts memory retention by up to 30 percent. Repetitive patterns seem to produce the best results for mindfulness, but don't place too many restrictions on your doodling. In the space below, unleash your doodling as you focus solely on the paper and the writing instrument moving across it. Don't judge the outcome for artistic merit; just enjoy the process.

PERMISSION FOR EXCESSIVE CELEBRATION

Throughout your day, pause whenever something good happens. In situations where you can, acknowledge the blessing with a small celebratory word (as simple as "good" or "thanks") or act (such as lifting up your palms or giving a thumbs-up). What will your celebration sign be?

Does the pause help you focus on the good in your life?

Too many people
go through

LIFE

without pausing to

ENJOY

what they have.

—David Gemmell

STAR REPORT

Take a night to lie under the sky and stargaze, without distractions. Sketch the stars in the arrangement they appear to you.

What new perspective(s) does stargazing give you?

MEDIA CLEANSE

Keep track of the media that you watch, read, and listen to throughout a typical day. Note how each affects your mood and your focus throughout the rest of the day, and ask yourself what you are consuming and why.

Media	Mood	Motivation

In today's rush,
we all think too much,
SEEK TOO MUCH,
want too much
and forget about
THE JOY
of just being.

—Eckhart Tolle

Anxiety is one

LITTLE TREE

in your forest.
Step back and look at the

WHOLE FOREST.

—Anonymous

THE WHOLE BEAUTIFUL PICTURE

Name in the circle below one especially nagging worry in your head right now. Then surround that circle with as many things as you can think of that you are grateful for in this moment. Does your worry fade away in this perspective?

COUNTDOWN TO CALM

Whenever you need grounding in the present, you can turn to your senses. An exercise called 5-4-3-2-1 will guide you anytime, anywhere. Simply identify:

5 sights you can see

4 things you can feel

3 sounds you can hear

2 smells you can pick out

1 taste reaching you (even if it's just a hint of your toothpaste or the aftertaste of coffee)

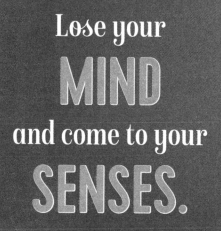

Lose your

MIND

and come to your

SENSES.

—Fritz Perls

Nature does not hurry,
yet everything is

ACCOMPLISHED.

–Lao Tzu

PRESENCE IN NATURE

Nature and mindfulness are perfect partners because spending time in nature brings so much potential to awaken the senses and align you with natural rhythms. How can you plan to soak in more nature today?

Sit near a window

Take a walk instead of a coffee break

Spend time gardening

Go on a gratitude walk

Sketch in nature

SHIFTING LANES

Everyday activities often become meditative as you slow down the pace. What can you move from the fast to the slow lane? Examples: eating meals, cleaning, yardwork, getting ready in the morning.

Fast Lane

Slow Lane

Never be in a hurry;
do everything
QUIETLY
and in a calm
SPIRIT.

—Saint Francis de Sales

We were

TOGETHER.

I forget the rest.

—Walt Whitman

BEING PRESENT FOR OTHERS

Look over your to-do list for today and cross out one thing that can wait. Replace that task with time set aside to devote to someone important in your life. How will you show your love and give your full attention?

LEAVING BEHIND THE *WHENS*

Too much time spent making wishes for the future can hold you back from all that is waiting for you in the now. Fill in the *when*s you find yourself saying in your head, then cross them out.

When I _____, life will be better.

When I _____, life will be better.

When I _____, life will be better.

Circle, highlight, surround with stars, whatever it takes to emphasize this thought below.

LIFE IS GOOD *NOW.*

Learn to enjoy the
SLICE OF LIFE
you experience, and life
turns out to be
WONDERFUL.

—Leo Babauta

Walk as if you are

KISSING

the earth with your feet.

—Thich Nhat Hanh

NO GOAL IN SIGHT

Find a place where you can walk without a destination or defined purpose in mind. Choose a location with boundaries that you know well enough to safely wander and wonder, to explore and discover more deeply. As you walk, consider the movements of your body and what you sense in the environment around you. How does it feel to wander without a goal? What do you find?

POINTS OF CONTACT

Wherever you are and in whatever position you are in, focus on the points of your body that come into contact with any kind of surface. Are your feet touching cold concrete or soft carpet? Or is your back sinking into the mattress? Where do you feel contact the strongest? Can you distribute weight more evenly if a contact feels too hard or a part of your body needs to release tension? Record your observations in words or sketches below.

Breathe and

RELEASE

anything that does not

serve you.

—Anonymous

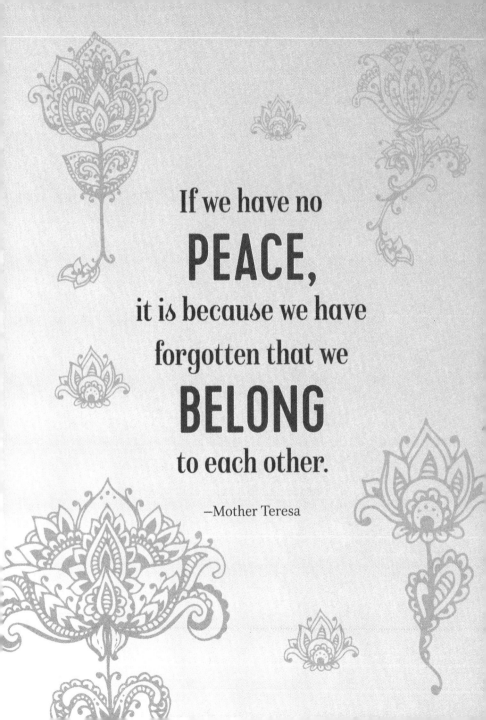

If we have no
PEACE,
it is because we have
forgotten that we
BELONG
to each other.

—Mother Teresa

KINDNESS IN MIND

Choose a person who somehow grabs your attention in the course of your day. Consider not what they're wearing or doing in particular, but focus on the truth that they are someone with hopes, dreams, and even frustrations—just like you. In your head, wish them a day filled with good things. What went through your mind, and how did you feel after those moments?

TURNING THE PAGE TO NOW

Is there a chapter in your life that you're holding on to that needs a conclusion? Even if there doesn't seem to be a resolution possible, write your own ending here.

Everything that has

A BEGINNING

has an ending. Make

YOUR PEACE

with that and all
will be well.

—Jack Kornfield

Learn
EVERYTHING
you can,
ANYTIME
you can, from
ANYONE
you can.

—Sarah Caldwell

FRESH FOCUS

In your experiences today, look for and record, through words or pictures, anything new you encounter. Be open to new tastes, sights, fragrances, sounds, and perspectives.

SENSING YOUR BREATH

Sit in a comfortable position, breathing naturally. Bring your focus to your breath, visualizing your inhalations as calming blue light entering your body and your exhalations as dark smoke leaving your body. After a series of breaths, go deeper to notice what your breath feels like moving through specific parts of your body: from your nose and mouth to your chest, belly, and beyond. How do you feel after this exercise?

Cleansed Energized Full

Clear Calm Enlightened

When you own your

BREATH,

nobody can steal your

PEACE.

–Anonymous

The butterfly
counts not months but
MOMENTS,
and has time enough.

–Rabindranath Tagore

WALKING MEDITATION

Take a slow, gratitude-filled walk in a natural place. As you open your senses to the gifts all around you, capture ten things that bring joy to your soul in the spaces below.

1. _____

2. _____

3. _____

4. _____

5. _____

6. _____

7. _____

8. _____

9. _____

10. _____

PLACE OF PEACE

Where is one place in your home that you can go to for peaceful retreat? Doesn't exist? Imagine what you want it to look like and make it happen. Draw the real or planned space below, highlighting the features of the room that induce calm.

HAPPINESS

not in another place,
but this place . . .
not for another hour, but

THIS HOUR.

—Walt Whitman

Your

CALM MIND

is the ultimate

WEAPON

against your

challenges.

—Bryant McGill

BUILDING IN RELEASE

Promise yourself three daily pockets of time (try 15 minutes each) when you can put aside everything "productive" to refresh your mind with a stroll or simply gazing out a window. What times work best for you and how will you savor the breaks?

A DEEPER LOOK

In your interactions today, focus on making eye contact with someone you care about. Keep it soft and inviting, not uncomfortable. Sketch the detail you see in and around the person's eyes in the space below.

The

QUESTION

is not what you

LOOK AT,

but what

YOU SEE.

–Henry David Thoreau

COLORING MEDITATION

Colored pencils or crayons can be meditation tools. As you color the letters and patterns on the next page, try to keep your mind on the action of coloring, not evaluating the results as you go. Feel the coloring implement in your hand. Listen to the sound as it glides over the paper. Watch the color transfer onto the page. If distracting thoughts pull you away from the moment, acknowledge them by releasing them in the space below. Then return to your coloring meditation.

After you've completed your meditation time, rip out the coloring page. Post the reminder somewhere you'll see it when your mind tends to fly off in unhealthy directions.

RIGHT HERE, RIGHT NOW